WITH JESUS
I am Kind

This book belongs to :

....

....

Copyrights

Copyright 2022 by Good News Meditations Kids - All rights reserved

This book or parts thereof may not be reproduced in any form, stored in any retrieval system, or transmitted in any form by any means—electronic, mechanical, photocopy, recording, or otherwise—without prior written permission of the copyright holder.

www.gnmkids.com

To receive print-ready pages from the coloring book version of this book, please go to gnmkids.com/free

"Happy Easter!" Eric's Sunday School teacher exclaimed with a smile. "Do you know why Easter is a special day?"

"Easter is the day we celebrate what Jesus did for us," Eric answered.

"Yes," his teacher said. "We are celebrating the most special gift Jesus ever gave us."
"What is that gift?" another pupil asked.

"Jesus took the punishment for the bad things everyone does," his teacher answered. "Everyone? Even bad people?" Eric asked. "Yes, and while doing that He was kind, even to people who were mean to Him. He can help you do the same," his teacher added.

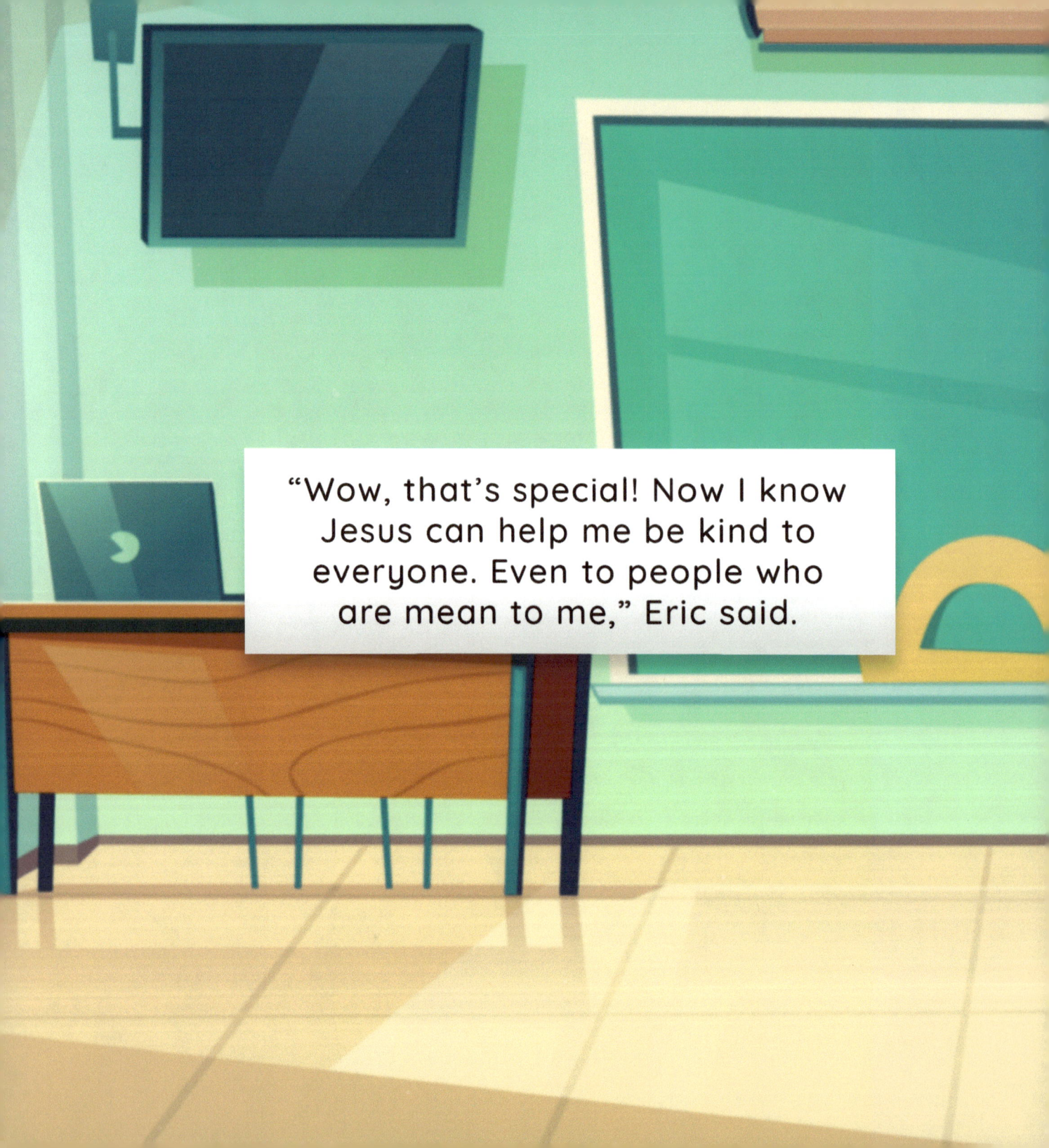
"Wow, that's special! Now I know Jesus can help me be kind to everyone. Even to people who are mean to me," Eric said.

After church, Eric and his family went to Fun Land for a picnic and to enjoy the rides. Eric and his dad got in line to ride the roller coaster.

While Eric waited, he began to open his giant golden Easter egg. He couldn't wait to eat the chocolate inside.
"That's cool!" a little boy behind him said. Suddenly, the boy grabbed the egg from Eric.

Before Eric could say anything, it was his turn to ride.

"I only have room for one more person," the man in charge said. Eric remembered the Sunday School lesson. "You can go first," he said to the boy who broke his egg.

Later that day, Eric and his dad saw the boy. "Thanks again," the boy said. "But why did you do that?" Eric grinned shyly. "Jesus helps us to be kind to everyone—even when someone… well, to everyone."

The boy looked surprised. "Wow, no one has ever been tha[t] kind to me... I'm really sorry I broke your egg," he said. "I forgive you," Eric replied. "And Happy Easter!"

The End.

Because Christ also suffered for us, leaving us an example, that ye should follow his steps: Who did no sin, neither was guile found in his mouth:Who, when he was reviled, reviled not again; when he suffered, he threatened not; but committed himself to him that judgeth righteously.

1 Peter 2:21-23

Author's note:

Thank you so much for reading this book. If you enjoyed this book, we would love it if you could leave a review and recommend it to a friend.

If there is anything you would like to share with us to help us improve this book, please go to gnmkids.com/feedback

Please checkout our other books

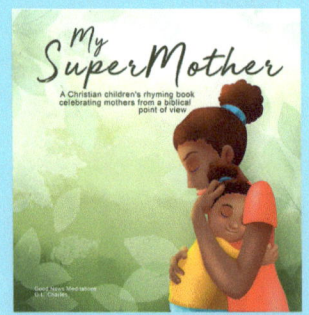

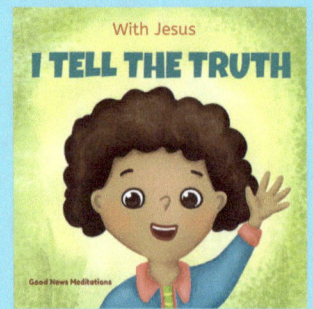

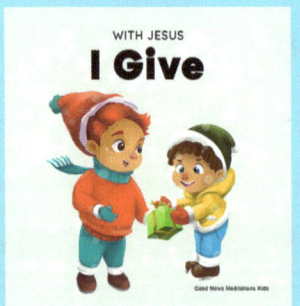
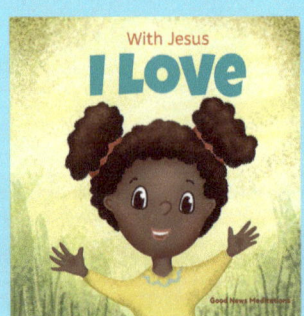
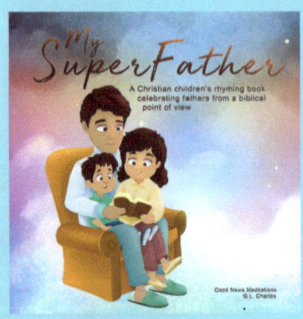

www.gnmkids.com

www.ingramcontent.com/pod-product-compliance
Lightning Source LLC
Chambersburg PA
CBHW042316280426
43673CB00080B/381